house beautiful
COLOR

house beautiful
COLOR

The Editors of
House Beautiful Magazine

Louis Oliver Gropp, Editor in Chief
Margaret Kennedy, Editor

Text by Sally Clark

HEARST BOOKS
NEW YORK

Library of Congress Cataloging-in-Publication Data

House Beautiful.

House beautiful color / the editors of House beautiful
magazine: text by Sally Clark.

p.   cm.

ISBN 0-688-10622-6

1. Color in interior decoration. I. House beautiful. II. Title.

III. Title: Color.

NK2115.5.C6C53 1993   92-39435

747'.94--dc20   CIP

Printed in Singapore

First Edition

1   2   3   4   5   6   7   8   9   10

Edited by Laurie Orseck

Designed by Michelle Wiener

Produced by Smallwood & Stewart, Inc., New York

CONTENTS

FOREWORD

As the pages of *House Beautiful* have demonstrated throughout the magazine's 96-year history, color is the most democratic of all the tools employed in the high art of decoration. This book, one of a series published by *House Beautiful* to assist you in your own decoration projects, is designed to show just how rich and available a resource color is. Whether primary hues straight from a child's crayon box, the elusive tints of gentle pastels, or strong contrasting tones, the colors chosen do more to set the mood of a room than anything else in it.

Always the child of light, color has more change built into it than any other decorative tool. This book shows the many ways in which it can be used, and will leave you with a keener understanding of color's vocabulary. It will help you appreciate the difference between a pure color like red and its many tones, each achieved by the addition of black or white.

Most importantly, it will give you permission to become brave with color: to use bright pink instead of white, for example, on walls that will house an art collection; or, conversely, to turn to the naturals, the tones of nature, for one of decoration's most classic approaches. The important thing is not the choice, but its rightness for you: what it does to the rooms in which you live, and for the people who live in them.

Louis Oliver Gropp
Editor in Chief

house beautiful
COLOR

INTRODUCTION

Color is the element of decoration that naturally invites superlatives: It is the most exciting, the most versatile, the most elevating component of design. It can also be the most intimidating. With so many colors on the charts, and so many decisions to make about where to put color in a room ~ on the walls, the furniture, the accessories ~ it is easy to become confused and discouraged. Most people shy away from the bright yellow or intense sky blue room they really want and settle instead for something they have decided is "safe."

This book is intended to banish that fear. That there are no hard and fast rules about color is apparent in the rooms that follow. Most were designed by professionals; the numerous ways in which they have chosen to use color provides an arsenal of ideas, which are discussed in the accompanying text. *House Beautiful* offers solutions for creating harmony in relation to texture, light, and tone, for using color to show off interior architecture, furniture, and all kinds of personal collections.

The book is conveniently organized into two sections. The first part is devoted to color schemes and combinations. True colors deals with pure color, as well as the infinite array of pastel tints and rich shades that can be derived from them. Next come the naturals, which take their colors from materials found in nature ~ wood, marble, sand, and clay. The dramatic value of classic light-dark pairings such as black and white is examined. And white, with its ability to change from setting to setting and its capacity to strongly affect mood, is explored in depth.

In the second part of the book the practical applications of color are addressed: the many ways in which paint assists in establishing the colored surfaces of a room; the role that fabric plays in filling out a color scheme; and the ways in which accents and accessories energize a room through color.

Every aspect of color is illustrated through profiles of homes across the country. The interiors chosen represent a range of styles, from traditional to cutting-edge contemporary. By studying them, borrowing from them, and adapting them, you can make color a force of beauty and self-expression in the decoration of your home.

chapter 1

TRUE COLORS

Perhaps the best advice about tackling color in decorating is designer Dorothy Draper's. "Above all," she reassured, "never be afraid of color." At a time when the paint shops' ready-mixed gallons were anemic pastels, Draper painted sitting rooms the deep green of magnolia leaves and swathed sofas in cyclamen-colored fabric. She was fearless. So was legendary designer Billy Baldwin. A client of his needed a backdrop for displaying a stunning collection of American abstract paintings. Baldwin supplied, not the expected art-gallery-white walls, but deep pink ones, the luscious color of raspberry ice. Today's professional colorists, the decorators and architects whose work appears on the pages that follow, enthusiastically carry on this colorful tradition. By incorporating lively hues and inventive combinations in their work, America's leading designers speak to what appears to be a national fondness for light-filled, clear colors. It is these colors, in their purest form, that have a great ability to stir the emotions: A red room is exciting, provocative; a green room is restful; a yellow room is as cheering as the sun. These are not clichés, but real effects made possible by the power of color.

A COLOR-DRENCHED WEEKEND HOUSE

The kelly green wicker chair (above) adds a summery note to the upholstered red-and-white-checked sofas and chairs in the living room.

In a house with expanses of glass, the colors of nature's vista become part of the interior scheme, as does the rich tapestry of green woodlands beyond the deck (opposite).

The vivid, pure colors of Henri Matisse light up the rooms of this house in the hilly woodlands of upstate New York. When color appears in its purest form, without black or white added, as the reds, greens, blues, and purples in these interiors, color experts describe the hues as saturated. Such a full-strength palette is not overwhelming in this developer's spec house because its architect, Byron Bell, chose white walls and natural wood floors as flexible neutral backgrounds that would go with any color scheme. The plan of the house is simple: two pavilions, one a public space with living, dining, and kitchen areas, the other a private space with two bedrooms, linked by a glassed-in passageway.

The primary colors of the living room come straight from a child's crayon box and impart an immediate sense of fun, perfect for a weekend place designed to buoy a city dweller's spirits. Generous areas of white ~ the walls and soaring gabled ceiling ~ help cool down the intensity of the furniture's vivid colors. Another stabilizing influence is the natural wood surfaces of the beams over-head and the board flooring below; the spruce floor turned a pink-orange color after a white stain was applied and rubbed off.

As emphatic as the colors is the geometric theme of checkerboards that animates the living room. As if echoing the grid of the panes in the French doors, the oversize red-and-white checked fabric on chairs and sofa

creates a striking pattern, as does the black-and-white rug, as bold as an American folk-art game board.

Lavender paint, inside and out, was Bell's choice of trim color for the house's numerous French doors. The architect believes the color has the mutable property of turning warm or cool depending on the colors and light around it. On sunny days, the outside trim turns blue; inside, it becomes a brilliant violet, a striking accent for any interior scheme. "It made the house come alive," he explains

Bell was so delighted with the design and decor once the building was completed that he bought the house as a country escape for his wife and himself.

With no dividing walls in the public wing of the house, living area and dining area flow into each other. Color and pattern become the defining factors in visually separating the two. In contrast to the brightly colored living room furniture (opposite), the two little octagonal tables and companion slat-back chairs in the dining area are painted buttermilk white (above). The rug in the dining area is a different geometric pattern from the one in the living room, though its effect is just as lively.

DEFINING A MANHATTAN LOFT WITH COLOR

In remodeling the loft into an open-plan apartment (opposite), architect Michael Rubin used two paint colors to distinguish the old space from the new: white for the original shell, saturated green for the newly added ceilings and walls. In the living room, the green stands up boldly to the black furniture (above). The leather chair trimmed in red and the green rocker are children's furniture.

The manner in which one full-bodied color can unify a large area is apparent in this New York City loft, where architect Michael Rubin painted walls green ~ "Jaguar green" ~ in the process of converting a huge industrial space into a home for a family of four.

To retain the factory-like character of the former printing plant, the architect kept the original shell ~ columns, ceiling, and exterior walls ~ intact. Into the core he inserted a luxurious kitchen of birch and Tennessee marble. On either side, he carved out a dining room, living room, and three bedrooms. A large, generously windowed area adjoining the kitchen forms a dining room and a passageway to the living room on one side, and a master suite on the other.

Running throughout the loft are the colors of the pale birch cabinets and the salmon pink of the marble. To complement these hues, Rubin knew he needed a paint color with character. He had to find one that would not dissolve in the strong sunlight that pours into the space through the big old factory windows on three sides of the apartment. And he had to find one gutsy enough to anchor the large interior ~ nearly 3,000 square feet, with 14½-foot ceilings ~ and form a distinctive complement to the other materials in the loft.

"What I learned by testing light colors against light colors was that everything seemed empty," the architect explains. It

Green is considered an emotionally calming color. That property is quite apparent in the master bedroom, where the forest-green walls and shoji-like glass screens create an atmosphere of almost oriental tranquility. The charcoal carpeting that runs through the living room and bedrooms is also used to upholster the birch-trimmed bookshelf in front of the glass screen.

All the materials and colors of the loft appear in the master bath, where the floor and tub trim are pink-veined marble and the vanity cabinet is birch (below left). Against well-defined colors of wood and marble, Benjamin Moore's Number 629 green paint shows off its neutral quality, "holding" the room together without grabbing the limelight. In one of the boys' rooms (below right), the green walls are a wonderful foil for the bright primary colors of the toys displayed on the shelves and the red, yellow, light and dark blue linens on the platform beds.

was at that point that he decided to paint the original exterior walls and columns white, and to find a darker color for all the new construction. The green cast of the frosted glass in the shoji-style screens between the rooms prompted him to experiment with green. In a test of three hues, he painted large sections of wall ~ experts agree this is the best way to choose paints. Benjamin Moore's Number 629 won. Says Rubin, "It's a cool green. It strikes a balance between blueness and yellowness. It's a committed kind of color, a very saturated green, and it's very soothing."

With its soft, muted quality, the shade stands up well to the gray and black colors Rubin selected for the loft's furnishings.

Charcoal gray carpeting runs through the living room and bedrooms. For the living room, Rubin designed a black leather sofa, then added an Alvar Aalto classic chair, upholstered in the bold zebra-patterned fabric Aalto originally specified. A geometric area rug in the room, designed by architect Charles Gwathmey, is another classic, chosen for its Art Deco palette of gray, maroon, cognac, and avocado.

The green walls also work in the rest of the loft. In fact, says Rubin, the color is so flexible that it is sometimes tempting to take it for granted as a neutral shade. "When you're in the space," he explains, "you're hardly aware that it's green."

UPDATING TRADITION
WITH OFFBEAT PASTELS

Pastel colors are always soothing. They are emotionally satisfying because of the associations they conjure up ~ the gentle colors of old-fashioned pink roses, of sweet peach ice cream and lavender satin dance slippers. On a wall or sofa, a soft pastel seduces the eye without being intrusive, warming up a room and often providing more definition to objects and surfaces than a white fabric or paint can.

The living room and bedroom featured here and on the next four pages show how arresting pastels can be, especially when used in unexpected combinations. Instead of a conventional scheme of baby blue or pink, which might have seemed too bedroom-like for a public space, the living room pairs periwinkle walls with pistachio-green club chairs. The unusual choices work together because they all share the same tonal value, the term designers use to describe the darkness or lightness of a color. (Adding black to a color creates dark tones, or shades. By contrast, the addition of white to a color creates tints.) All the tones in the room seem to have a slightly ephemeral quality, turning from quite definite pastel shades to the barest hint of color depending on the way daylight and lamplight strike them. Here the sheen of some of the surfaces and fabrics ~ the chintz on the chairs, the damask on the sofa, for example ~ contributes a pearly quality that adds to the elusive effect of these pastels. To tie the room's architectural details together, the mantel, French doors, and other woodwork were painted porcelain white. Finally, spots of contrasting color were used to energize the space: brown and coral accent pillows, black candlestick lamps, and burnished accessories and ornaments.

In the bedroom, chartreuse on the walls is a delightful surprise and as pleasingly offbeat as the periwinkle color in the living room. Lettuce-green curtains of glazed chintz emphasize the green glow.

On a practical note, painting walls unusual colors that will always be noticed tends to "fill" them up and eliminates the need for a strong showing of paintings and other artwork. That can be advantageous when working on a limited decorating budget.

Resting on the pistachio-colored armchair, a large pillow covered in a periwinkle cotton chintz repeats the pretty pastel color of the walls in the living room. The use of mostly solid colors adds to the serene quality of the setting; another pillow covered in brown-and-white toile de Jouy is one of the few patterns in the room.

Informal elegance is the
watchword in the living
room, where the carpeting
is rough sisal and the
windows are curtainless.
The accessories are as
quirky as the pistachio
and periwinkle palette.
Sly touches of glamour
wink from all sides,
including an antique
screen, and on the mantel
a nineteenth-century
watercolor in a gold frame.

Mahogany furniture would have been over-powering in this free-spirited pastel living room. The pale pine armoire (right) and chic pedestal dining table in birch (below) are better choices for the soft color schemes. Dining chairs are covered in cotton ticking with a khaki stripe.

Dressed in a blue-and-white duvet with a floral pattern on one side and crisp stripes on the other, the pencil-post bed lends a romantic old-fashioned air to the bedroom (opposite). Picking up the greenish cast of the chartreuse walls is a rattan bedside table, stained sage green.

THE VOCABULARY OF COLOR

A few basic terms can go a long way in understanding the language of color used by designers and architects:

The Color Wheel: This is the traditional vehicle for representing the colors of the spectrum and their relationship to each other. The color wheel was first devised by Sir Isaac Newton. By bending light through a prism, Newton discovered that the resulting colors formed a spectrum. He then arranged those colors in a circle: red, orange, yellow, green, blue, purple, returning to red.

Complementary Colors: Colors that appear opposite each other on the color wheel ~ for example, red and green, blue and yellow. The energy they set off when paired in a design scheme creates vibrant results.

Analogous Colors: Colors that are next to each other on the color wheel. Teaming analogous colors ~ red and orange, green and blue ~ creates visual harmony in a room.

Hue: In general usage, the words color and hue are interchangeable. However, to color experts, hue also has the more precise meaning of indicating the specific attribute of a color ~ for example, red with a bluish hue, or green with a yellowish hue.

Value: The lightness or darkness of a color.

Saturation: The purity or brightness of a color. A highly saturated color reads bright and clear. By contrast, a less saturated color will appear gray or muted.

Tone: A pure color that has been modified

Color unbottled: Light streaming through the window releases the beauty of colored glass in a collection of decanters and containers arranged by designer Jorge Letelier.

by the addition of black or white. Dark tones, or shades, result from mixing a saturated color with gray or black. Light tones, or tints, are achieved by mixing a saturated color with white.

The dazzling blues and
greens of a collection of
antique majolica gave
designer Greg Jordan the
cue for the other intense
colors in a sunroom: an
armoire lacquered deep
green and seating covered
in two tones of blue ~
ultramarine and delft
(left and below). The
floorboards, striped in
alternating light and dark
stains, are a lively detail
that keeps the assemblage
of dark blue chairs from
looking too heavy.

Famous for artfully mixing prints, designer Mario Buatta relies on his unerring color sense. In this living room (right), the floral curtain and checked table skirt he chose strike a harmonious balance because of their shared tones of rose and apple green.

Instead of a sedate stripe, which would be the traditional choice for covering the seat of a Hepplewhite-style side chair, designer Robert Currie opted for a colorful plaid (below). The overscale yellow-and-red geometric is a jazzy counterpoint to the classic mahogany furniture and matte brown walls.

A personal collection makes even more of an impact when pieces are the same color ~ in this case, a massed display of Arts and Crafts pottery in vibrant celadon in designer Jorge Letelier's home (opposite).

chapter 2

THE NATURALS

The hues inherent in nature comprise one of the most popular color groups in decorating. Wood, stone, clay, quarry tile, marble, glass, steel ~ by virtue of their unique combination of color and textures, these surfaces contribute effortlessly to the total look of a room. The subtle tones of natural materials are restful: the mellow, warm browns of wood, the familiar putties and grays of stone, the textured beiges of rattan and cane, the comforting creams of natural cotton and linen. For the decorator, the naturals are an attractive and useful design tool because they are neutral, making them an excellent foil for bolder colors and treatments. When several naturals are used together, they can create an exciting tableau of muted colors and textures. A room full of naturals has the subtlety of a beautiful piece of Scottish tweed and is as fascinating to the eye as a misty day at the beach where sand, stone, and driftwood prevail.

Always fresh to look at and easy to live with, the naturals are often the best choice as a design investment for they are classics that never go out of style. That is not always true of some colors, which may be the last word in fashion one year and definitely "out" the next. The naturals stand firm on the high ground of style, providing a timeless environment of tranquility and comfort.

IN HARMONY
WITH NATURE

John Saladino is a designer who savors the subtleness of color. His clients, the owners of this house, are a couple with a passion for natural materials, barn construction, and Shaker cabinetry. The result of their three-year collaboration is this rambling weekend house hugging the Long Island dunes, a structure that combines the unfinished look of an old barn with a strain of luxury reminiscent of the Arts and Crafts movement. For Saladino it was the perfect place to create the rooms he loves: interiors with deliberately utilitarian architectural finishes filled with antiques and quietly sumptuous furniture covered in silks, velvets, and linens.

Much of the two-year process of constructing the 12,000-square-foot house was devoted to aging the materials to get the exact colorations Saladino wanted. The posts and beams for the living room and kitchen were left to stand outside for a year until sun and rain had weathered the hickory, oak, and pine timbers. The scratch-coat plaster walls that are Saladino's signature also took time. (The scratch coat is the construction layer over which the final plasterwork is customarily applied. But because of its rough, tactile quality and its natural color of putty with a slightly green cast, Saladino often leaves the scratch

coat exposed. This requires extremely careful application so that it looks as smart as finished plaster.) When completed, the walls created a shell in which the colors ranged between beige and the gray-green of of celadon pottery. The final effect was of a seamless envelope of soft neutrals.

Into these spaces Saladino introduced furniture of his own design, covered in fabrics in such colors as periwinkle, celadon, and copper. He calls these "nuance" colors ~ "those that are metamorphic, that don't reveal themselves immediately." They vary from room to room and change with the light. With this in mind, the designer selected the upholstery colors and positioned the furniture according to the way sunlight hits each room. In the living room, for example, furniture near a huge window is done in deeper tones; in less sunny parts of the room, the fabrics are in lighter tones.

Throughout the house, one color is constant: the teal blue paint on all the inside window frames. It might be a reference to the house's American design roots ~ it is a typical Shaker color ~ or it might be a reminder of the sea and sky beyond the windows. In Saladino's hands color is always an intriguing puzzle in which possibilities are implied, never pinned down.

Pale tones in the entrance hall are based on natural materials: scratch-coat plaster walls and floors of Mexican volcanic stone, both left in an untreated state. Stairs are quarter-sawn white oak. The hand-forged metalwork throughout the house, including the banister, was allowed to turn to a rusted patina in the seaside air, then sealed to capture its oxidized color.

39

"The fabrics are very
elegant and the rest of the
room is throwaway
chic," says head designer
Benjamin Noriega-Ortiz
about the living room's
contrast between the
barn-like construction
and refined upholstery in
lilting pastels (left). The
sofa is covered in celadon
cotton velvet, with
pillows in pink and
beige silk. The color of
the wool tapestry on a
chair near the fireplace
hovers between violet
and lavender. Fine
American antiques, such
as one of a pair of Queen
Anne mirrors (above),
stand out in each room.

41

In the open kitchen, the use of dark colors such as the mirror-shiny black granite on the counters and backsplash and teal paint on the Shaker-style cabinets makes the area appear to recede from the adjacent dining room. Indeed, this is a kitchen meant to serve, then fade into the background when meals are done.

Shaker-style cabinetry throughout the house was custom-made. The superb storage wall in the master suite dressing room, with its ruddy natural cherrywood surface, stands out against walls and ceiling finished in Pratt & Lambert's "Seed Pearl" paint. The colors of the nineteenth-century Bessarabian rug blend beautifully with the wood.

A guest bedroom is a study in hazy blue nuance colors (below). The wood-beamed ceiling and Shaker-style chest of drawers continue the house's neutral theme. The walls and ceiling are painted with Pratt & Lambert's "Smoke Ring."

Metallic colors make frequent appearances, in objects such as a quilted pillow covered in silk the color of a shiny copper coin (top); an oxidized coppper Trilogy lamp designed by Saladino (above); and an antique brass dressing table (opposite).

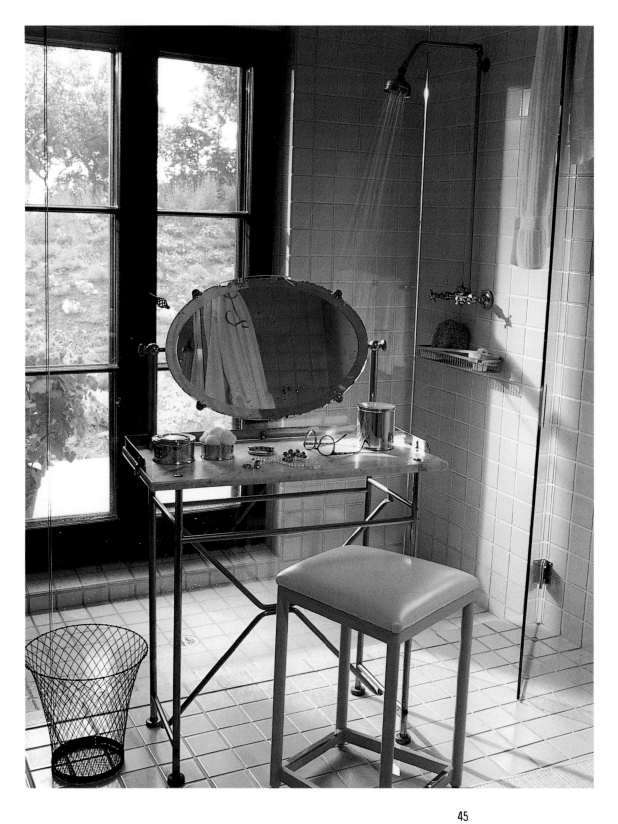

Enclosed in an octagonal wing, the library is a wonderfully warm room by virtue of its unique shape. The designer improved the coziness by applying an inky stain called Tetra Negra to redwood walls ~ "the color Caravaggio and Titian used in the background of their paintings, a shade that is neither black nor brown," says designer Noriega-Ortiz. Next to the dense shadowiness of the walls, the pale tones of the antique oriental carpet and sofa have a topaz shimmer. The sofa fabric is pale green linen; oxidized copper studs outline the sofa arms.

SHADES OF A
RESTFUL HOUSE

Under the brilliant southern California sun the landscape of Palm Springs is as flamboyantly colored as the plumage of a tropical bird. Grass and trees are verdant. Walled gardens lush with scarlet bougainvillaea blossoms are framed against the violet haze of the surrounding mountains. "There is so much color outside," says Los Angeles designer Ron Wilson, "that you don't need any more of it inside." So in planning his weekend house, Wilson decided to let an array of natural materials mandate a neutral scheme. Cream, white, buff, honey, and terracotta: These are the tranquil colors of his desert getaway. The rooms are restful, but never visually static, thanks to an abundance of textures and finishes that enhance and enrich the building's Mediterranean character.

"Mediterranean houses are my first love," says the designer. He literally performed the sow's-ear-to-silk-purse trick, turning a mostly demolished 1950s house that once stood on the site into a Mediterranean-style complex completely enclosed by a high wall. Behind the wall, "on the footprint of the old foundation," he constructed a three-bedroom main house. Close to the street, just behind the wall, he designed a separate guest house, connected to the main house by a 70-foot loggia. Large modern windows give every room a view of the brilliantly colored flower garden and turquoise pool outside. "Part of what I consider color in this house comes from the garden," Wilson explains.

The attention to texture began with the architecture. Thick, thick plaster walls ("very Mediterranean," says Wilson) were painted rich cream, a color the designer calls cottage white. Ceiling beams and doors turned a honey glow in a whitewash process that involved tinting sealer with a dash of white paint before brushing it on the raw wood. Terracotta tile floors lend a russet flush to all the rooms.

Against the neutral background Wilson set in place plump, somewhat overscale furniture, covering it in natural-textured cream linen and cotton. The few accessories throughout the house are also neutral: wicker baskets, American Indian leather gourds, and woven rugs. And everywhere are the tactile surfaces of reed, mellow wood, matte plaster, and nubby cotton and linen textiles. "It's all very calming," says the designer. He often works with bright colors, but he admits he prefers the subtlety of natural tones as a background for himself and his favorite house guests, whom he considers quite colorful enough.

"It's all buff," says designer Ron Wilson of his Palm Springs weekend house (opposite). Underscoring the retreat's Mediterranean look are old plaster columns that define the entryway, a 1930s ceiling motif turned into an over-the-door decoration, and cool terracotta tiles on the floor.

49

In the living room Wilson arranged a series of woven textures in beiges and honey browns that give an almost rhythmic energy to the space. They include the split-wood bases of the Mexican wraparound chairs and the rough-textured wall hanging of canvas strips. The designer appropriated the Tuscan-looking fireplace from the Mediterranean-style houses built in southern California in the 1920s and 1930s.

The natural tones in the dining room progress from light to dark, moving from the white canvas pillows to cream walls to the beige travertine table to the deep browns of the Mexican pigskin chairs. This neutral room, in which dinner guests are pampered by chairs big enough for two, invites a grand display of color in the table settings, flowers, and food. A wall of French doors opens to the terrace; the garden, planted with oleander and roses, is another source of color, visible from every window.

The sybaritic bathroom feels like an outdoor oasis with its pine rafters and deep bay window. The black cabinet under the vanity is a dramatic contrast to the neutral pale browns of tiles and rafters. The rows of drawers and shelves are covered with licorice-colored grass cloth wall-covering, a sturdy material that stands up well in humid conditions. Shielded by the garden wall, the house is free of window coverings that might interfere with the outdoor views.

DRAWING INSPIRATION
FROM NATURE

Antique and reproduction American country furniture go comfortably together because they often share the same neutral colors. This cupboard and table display old, nicely faded painted finishes; the chair has "aged" thanks to the application of paint in a historic putty color.

The naturals are decorating's longest-running colors. From the quarry tile floors of the Italian Mediterranean farmhouse to the wood-and-rice-paper Japanese domicile, it is the tones of the naturals that have always dominated.

Today the naturals have achieved the status of modern classics, recognized as the essential elements of a certain contemporary ~ and thoroughly American ~ decorating style. The style may involve antique or modern furniture, or an eclectic mix of the two, but its overall effect is smartly tailored and serenely neutral in color. Albert Hadley, Ward Bennett, and John Saladino are the East Coast masters of this look. On the West Coast, the naturals have inspired the "California" style, characterized by natural-colored cotton and linen fabrics; pale, often bleached woods; and beige and cream marble and ceramic surfaces. Often the only color in these rooms is the green of plants. In borrowing generously from nature for their interiors, California designers skillfully achieve the balance so essential for the West Coast's enviable indoor-outdoor way of living.

Texture is the element that ensures vitality when decorating with naturals. A room of beiges, creams, and whites will never be bland if it is assembled with a variety of textured surfaces in its architectural finishes and furnishings.

Designers Peter Shelton and Lee Mindel used off-white tones and natural materials to give a flowing feeling to a Manhattan apartment. Several major elements in the living room are the color of Devonshire cream: an envelope of white paint on walls and ceiling, creamy upholstery fabrics, and a custom V'Soske rug. To keep the whiteness as seamless as possible, the designers selected glass for the tabletops; its transparency makes it an ideal surface in rooms where airiness is called for. The round table in the middle of the living room displays books and a collection of stoneware vases (above). At the far end of the room a glass coffee table sits between comfortable chairs with tufted backs (below).

In several rooms in the home of Connecticut antiques collector Pat Guthman, who specializes in eighteenth-century American furniture, the only colors are the mellowed tones of old wood, ceramics, and metalwork. The house is actually new, but to give it an old look and complement her stellar collection, the owner added architectural details as old as the furniture; the wooden archways are the most striking examples.

In the dining room of designer Sheila Camera Kotur's 1790 New England house, the reigning colors are gradations of browns, from the orange tinge of the old tavern table to the madder-brown slat-back chairs (below). The unpainted woodwork and bare floors are pine.

A stone chimney (left) and its taupe tones dictated this room's country style and muted color scheme. Natural-colored reedy textures underscore the rustic theme: a sisal rug, an old hickory chair, and a new rattan one. The French screen is a study in grayish beige and terracotta tones.

chapter 3

LIGHTS AND DARKS

The combination of light and dark is one of the most dramatic conceits in design. Light colors juxtaposed with blacks, steel grays, and black-browns create a striking effect because of the sharp contrast in values. (Light hues tend to advance, while darks recede.) Since classical times, designers have exploited the pairing to achieve dramatic results. Black and white is the most basic example of this combination. White has the highest light value, black the lowest. Color experts describe the two as achromatic colors because they have no particular hue. But the visual tension of the two together can be as exciting as a brilliant red room ~ especially when strong geometric shapes figure in the design. Other light and dark combinations are also powerful: Navy and white and teak brown and white are but two examples. And cream and the most fragile of pale pastel tints can be striking when paired with black and almost-black colors.

As the paintings of Piet Mondrian illustrate so vividly, black and white work well when teamed with clear, bright, primary colors. But in decorating, as in art, the added colors must be used sparingly to retain the high drama of the contrasting lights and darks.

EBONY AND IVORY

The contrast of black and white is so arresting to Linda Banks, a Connecticut architect and designer, that there was no question of any other color scheme when she decided to revamp her 1920s colonial house. As part of an extensive renovation to modernize the kitchen, Banks took down walls and created one large space with areas for sitting and dining opening off the kitchen. The new kitchen is in neutral creams and beige tints. To create a bold contrast, she decorated the living room area in an ebony-and-ivory juxtaposition of color and pattern.

As a designer, Banks is fascinated with the qualities of opaqueness and transparency in color, an interest that influenced her treatment of the architectural backgrounds in her home. In order to display to full advantage the blacks and whites she loves, she opted for a neutral background, extending the paint colors of the kitchen walls and floor into the rest of the space. To achieve the pale backdrop she was after, she chose a paint color for the walls that is neither beige nor cream, but a surprising face-powder pink ~ a soft color that changes with the light. Woodwork was painted a chalk white. At certain times of day, against the white trim, the blush-tinted walls seem almost sheer. The floor also has a gauzy quality: The old floor-

All the architecture is done in neutral tones so that it serves as a stage set for the graphic black-and-white furnishings. In the living room, the boldly striped valance crowning the multipaned window, an ebony-shaded lamp, and a graceful black pedestal table next to the sofa create much of the room's drama.

boards were stripped, then several applications of transparent stains and paint were applied in a diamond pattern of alternating cream and honey-toned squares. Tiny black painted squares punctuate the pattern. The floor, Banks explains, now has "an elusive tissue-paper fineness."

The illusion of sheerness in walls and floor became even more pronounced when the rooms were completely decorated. Banks chose strong sculptural shapes for the furniture. Decked in elegant black and white, it stands out boldly while the floor and walls almost melt away. For a wing chair and another chair with exaggerated high arms, Banks chose an overscale printed cotton. Black piping was added, like an illustrator's outline, to emphasize the furniture's sinuous forms. The other fabric in the room is a sharp graphic counterpoint to the print: black-and-white awning stripes at the windows. In this space without walls, four metal chairs define the dining area. So curved are their scroll-back forms that, in the pale room, the chairs take on the quality of sculpture. The accessories, with their strong shapes ~ a sunburst mirror, an urn lamp with paper shade, a winged figurine ~ almost look like silhouetted paper cutouts against the pale walls.

The paint applied to the walls of the living and dining area is Benjamin Moore's Number 1009, a translucent face-powder color. Against the blush tint, the metal chairs and dining table stand out as bold, sculptural outlines.

Upholstered in rice-colored cotton, the camel-back sofa is a pale foil for an arrangement of black and steel-gray accessories ~ a modern lamp, a winged figurine, and the frame on a painting by artist Elaine Anthony.

When a black-and-white print is as strong as the cotton fabric used on these chairs, little other pattern is needed to make a room snap together. The overall effect is clean, crisp, and dramatic.

REINVENTING
THE MODERNIST CANVAS

"Drop-dead white" is the way architect Mark McInturff describes the paint color he chose for the walls of this Washington, D.C., house. "We wanted uniform cool whites to play all the other elements against. The materials were doing the talking," he explains.

McInturff's clients, a European couple, have a penchant for smart modern rooms. The architect enlarged and reconfigured the house, a 1960s split-level, then followed the modernist taste of the homeowners in his color choices. The palette is straight from Mondrian's canvases: light and dark neutrals jolted by primary hues. The light neutrals are the white walls and pale bleached oak floors. The darks are the reddish-brown polished mahogany of the cabinets and window casements in every room. The architect revved up the design with flashes of silver ~ a suspended aluminum ceiling in the living room and aluminum sheathing on a hall wall. The interaction of aluminum and mahogany establishes another contrast of light and dark surfaces that animates the design.

Contemporary French furniture is done in black and primary hues. The living room rug, designed by the architect, features the same light and dark contrasts of neutrals and primaries as the rooms. A spirited assortment of pillows in primary colors and black-and-white dalmatian spots is a final fillip of contrasting values.

The checkerboard rug in the hallway (opposite) is a prelude to the theme of light-and-dark contrasts throughout the house. The theme is picked up again in the black-and-white spotted pillows in the living room, and even in a gold horse weathervane seen against a backdrop of dark woods (above).

65

Separated from the living room by a partial wall, the dining room has sliding doors that can close it off completely. Benjamin Moore's "Decorator White" on the walls and a bleached treatment on the oak floors provide a pale setting for the cherry-colored leather chairs and table of ebonized ash.

With its aluminum ceiling, the new living room just beyond is generously scaled and minimally detailed. Very little color was used on the architectural surfaces, allowing the bold pieces of furniture to dominate. The electric blue color of the couches is repeated on the custom rug, designed by the architect.

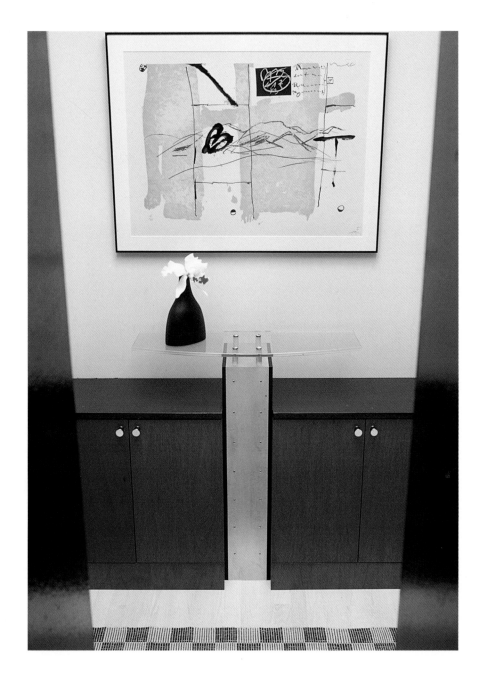

The playful design of the area rug (opposite) includes colored markers to designate where the coffee table legs sit; its squiggly grid is borrowed from the tabletop.

Lights and darks are carefully orchestrated in the entrance hall (above), right down to the white orchid in the black vase.

THE CLASSIC THEMES

Black-and-white rooms always appear on the cutting edge of modernity, yet the combination is one of the most ancient. Surviving examples of black-and-white mosaic floors ~ the linoleum of the ancient Roman world ~ display exciting geometric patterns worked from stone and marble chips. In the seventeenth century, the Dutch paved the ground-floor rooms of splendid houses with black-and-white marble squares.

The light-dark pairing is also one of the most graphically arresting in decorating. Always crisp and tailored, it is much more cerebral than emotional. That makes it a fine choice for public rooms. A black-and-white room always seems "alive" because of the constant play between lights and dark solids ~ a hallway with a checkerboard marble floor, for example, never looks empty; the pattern animates the space and anticipates human activity.

The lights and darks are a less likely combination for private rooms. Certainly black and white does not immediately telegraph either coziness or romance. However, the addition of a color ~ a brilliant scarlet, mandarin orange, or shocking pink ~ instantly warms up the light-dark scheme so that it is personal and inviting for a bedroom or library. The lights and darks also become very romantic in rooms where humble cottage fabrics predominate, such as brown-and-white cotton checks or black-and-white French toile.

Zebra patterns have long been favored by decorators for the dramatic contrasts they inject in a room. Designer David Salomon got a striking effect by hanging a reproduction of George Stubbs' 1763 painting "Zebra" in a room decorated in bright exotic colors.

Sometimes a dash of light-and-dark pattern will give a room just the right amount of visual tension. That is why decorators like zebra stripes, dalmatian spots, and herringbone stripes: Fabrics with these light-dark patterns are ideal for covering a chair or a few decorative pillows that will inject a bit of vitality into any interior design scheme. With positive-negative geometrics, a little goes a long way.

70

Painting any surface white makes it advance toward the eye. This fireplace, designed as the focal point of the living room by architect Mark Simon, is striking because of its temple shape; its white color, in contrast to the other hues in the room, makes it seem to zoom forward.

The dark taupe tones of the walls and chair backs are a striking contrast to the light-ground print in a room designed by Robert Currie (above). By reserving the print for the more visible front of the wing chairs, the designer followed an eighteenth-century upholstery technique for applying then-costly printed fabrics. But the twentieth-century black-and-white photographs on the walls depart completely from traditional period decor.

To solve the design dilemma for a couple with decidedly different tastes ~ she loves color, he is mad for black and white ~ Washington, D.C., designer David Mitchell used black and white in the main pieces, then spiked them up with colorful accessories (opposite). Result: a compromise that made both clients happy.

chapter 4

CHANGEABLE WHITES

Of all decorating colors, white may be the most intriguing because it is so changeable, so chameleon-like. White is naive ~ picture a milk-white farmhouse interior; yet it is worldly ~ imagine an eighteenth-century English dining room in cream, offset with Robert Adam motifs. It is innocent, it is sophisticated. It is the essence of simplicity, yet it is frankly luxurious. Technically, white is an achromatic color, meaning that it lacks distinctive hue. Highly reflective, it has a luminosity that makes it a fine choice for rooms in which an airy quality is desired. Emotionally, white is uplifting. Traditionally associated with the spiritual, it inspires serene, tranquil feelings.

The range of white tones is enormous. It runs from bluish, such as chalk white, to yellowish, such as cream. It can be warmed with a tint of pink, or, with a spritz of black, it can go to a cool oyster. Perhaps most alluring is the white-on-white room, in which myriad tones of white are combined to achieve a soft-edged richness. The white-on-white room is beguiling, inviting the eye to discover its elements gradually. Whether it is in a cottage or a townhouse, the all-white room is romantic, a flight of fancy from the practical concerns of day-to-day living.

WHITE ON WHITE ON WHITE

Cream white. Ivory white. Oyster white. White white. New York designer Vicente Wolf has used them all, in projects ranging from a spare Manhattan loft to a traditional Maryland house. These interiors, completed over the last few years, all bear a signature Wolf style: idiosyncratic spaces furnished with an eclectic combination of contemporary upholstery and offbeat old pieces, belonging to no identifiable design period ~ and always white.

"I see white as a canvas," says the designer, who is fascinated by the mutable property of the color. "White is really not a color. It's a chameleon depending on what you put with it."

In the beach house shown here, several creamy colors are always at work. The owners, a couple with two children, wanted white rooms to reflect the light of the Long Island shore. They also wanted an overall feeling of airiness and lightheartedness.

The designer began by transforming walls and ceiling into a pale shell. He chose ivory instead of pure white paint to predominate ~ its yellow property cuts down on glare and prevents rooms from looking burned out in the summer sun. The color was custom-mixed to blend with the cream-colored silk and wool curtains designed to hang to the floor at all the glass doors in the house. Although Wolf usually paints the ceiling two shades lighter than the walls in most of his projects (cast shadows make ceilings appear darker), he did not this time because the ceilings were so high.

The living room sofa is covered with cream-colored linen. To reinforce the seamless whiteness, the designer brought the sofa frame down low to the floor and had all the legs of the other seating upholstered or painted white as well. Once bleached, the wood floors took on a pale sheen. White vinyl, a practical idea for the beach, covers chairs in the dining area as well as the stools at the snack counter.

To inject the house with the warmth he thought it needed, Wolf carefully placed chairs and objects with well-worn finishes against the cream walls. By scouring local shops, he came up with an assortment of rough wood pieces ~ a Shaker chair, an old bench, some pieces from the Southwest ~ all bits of Americana that are a nod to Eastern Long Island's farm heritage and that "humanize" the ivory rooms.

The clients loved it.

The golden light that bathes Eastern Long Island in late summer glows in the foyer. The walls are painted ivory, not bright white, to avoid glare. The color is sympathetic to the mellow wood tones of the vintage chair and bench.

The core of the house, a spacious area where living room, dining room, and kitchen open into each other, is a collage of whites. In this cloud-like environment, Wolf limited the colors of the accessories to natural pale brown tones. A few beige-and-white striped pillows lend a bit of definition to the high-back L-shaped sofa (opposite). Beige surfaces are repeated on the wood trough and candlesticks on the coffee table (above left), and the stoneware bowl on the snack counter (above right). The only permanent colors in the room are the blues and greens in the contemporary photograph of an old building; in the all-white room, the photo looks like a slightly surreal window on the outside world.

BRINGING A SUN-WASHED FANTASY TO LIFE

Slipcovers made of white cotton duck and organdy are attached to the metal chairs with flirty spaghetti-strap ties. Bands of gold and cording accent the sofa pillows (above).

With its billowing white organdy curtains, the dining room could be a breezy pavilion in the Caribbean or on a Greek island (opposite).

"Whitewashed" was a word that kept popping up in conversations between designer Nancy Braithwaite and the owner of this 1920s Mediterranean-style house in Atlanta. "She was very articulate about what she wanted her house to feel like ~ a little like Capri, a little like the Caribbean, a little like *Out of Africa*," says the designer about her client.

Braithwaite, who dislikes decorating formulas, ushered in elements of surprise in a basic color plan of whites and "baby tints of color ~ soft blues, soft pinks." In some rooms, walls became white and fabrics with soft tints of color went on the upholstery. In other rooms, the process was reversed ~ soft tint on the walls and whites on furniture and curtains. Playing white surfaces against tints gave the interiors dimension and avoided the empty look all-white rooms sometimes have.

In the living room, Pratt & Lambert "Pearly Gates," a white paint with a hint of pink, was chosen for the walls. Pale, pale pink fabric was used on the two sofas, and even more pink tints were layered on with the decorative pillows she lavished on the sofas ~ "silks in every shade from peach to lavender." The remaining upholstery is covered in chalk white ~ linen on the club chairs and cotton duck on the 54-inch-square custom ottoman.

Pale lemon turned the master bedroom into a semitropical space that becomes gold

in the afternoon sun. Lavender-blue tint was the choice for the guest bedroom. The den became a glimmering confection when the walls and ceiling were painted silver with powdered paints.

The filmy white light streaming through the windows throughout the house comes courtesy of yards and yards of white organdy curtains. In the dining room, the designer indulged one of the owner's self-confessed "wild" fantasies and trimmed the drapes with hand-screened gilt borders; the diaphanous panels turn the space into a romantic summerhouse. For the living room, she added a hem treatment of heavy cream fringe, which forces the sheer fabric to stand away from the windows. The curtains seem to puff up and billow as if blown by unseen gusts of air.

In the guest room, a pale blue tint was applied to the walls (opposite). To achieve a similar effect for the curtains, the designer used double panels of organdy, one white and one powder blue. The bed is frothed with white organdy hangings and fresh white linens. In contrast to the room's sky-and-clouds scheme are the dark browns of a family portrait (above left).

Painted pale yellow, the master bedroom has a grand Mediterranean-style mantel (above right). The fireplace surround was painted beige-pink faux marbre to soften its appearance.

Beams in the living room were bleached to a dusty white that blends with the wall color, a white with a rosy blush. In this subtly colored environment, the designer wanted the 100-inch-long sofas to blend softly. After an extensive search for an upholstery fabric tinted a very gentle pink, she finally chose a pale rose-colored linen and cotton. For a bit of sparkle, a gold border was hand-screened on the oversize ottoman upholstered in cotton.

In the tiny den, designer
and owner pulled out all
the stops for a fantasy
look. Silvering the walls
and ceiling blurred the
edges of the room and
gave it the illusion of a
larger space. Fabric in
the barest whisper of
peach-pink covers the
sofa and was applied at
the edges of the inexpen-
sive matchstick blinds at
the window. As a fanci-
ful finishing touch, the
sofa is piled with Indian
pillows embroidered with
tiny silver mirrors.

THE PERFECT BACKDROP

If black is the absence of color, white is a mixture of all colors. In his experiments with prisms and light, Sir Isaac Newton was the first to identify the fact that white light contains all colors. This accounts for the complexity of white and its ability to change subtly depending on the other colors that are put with it. As designer Vicente Wolf points out, "Peach with white is very sweet, but black with white becomes stark. White is like a black dress you can dress up or down."

In doing up a white-on-white room, there is much less worry about matching colors, since whites of different tones are very sympathetic to one another. The layering of whites in all-white rooms tends to make the edges of furniture and accessories blur. If almost everything in the room is white, the result can be charming, and slight imperfections of scale, quality, or workmanship will not mar the effect. That would be less true in a tone-on-tone room of, say, red, which would require an experienced hand to pull off.

Another scheme that is fairly easy for the nonprofessional designer is the white room with upholstery or curtains done in a printed fabric on a white ground. A white ground makes floral prints look their most lush, while checks, stripes, and toile prints on white have a timeless charm. Against walls painted white, these fabrics create an effect that is classic and rich looking.

Except for the polished brown woodwork in this 1880s room, a medley of white tones is at work, ranging from pale ivory to creamier tones leaning toward yellow (above). Sleek glass and silver vessels juxtaposed with rough branches mingle with two unmatched styles of cream-colored china. A multiplicity of textures animates the tone-on-tone scheme.

Architect Michael Rex evoked the past when he chose white materials ~ tile, cabinets, appliances ~ in remodeling the kitchen of an 1885 farmhouse (opposite). The pitched ceiling is new, but its tongue-and-groove paneling, painted the color of fresh cream, is true to the period of the old house. Aqua walls set off the cream-colored woodwork.

In a serene bedroom with white ceiling and walls, John Saladino relies on sensual white textures ~ a plush wool rug and a *luxurious bedcover of quilted silken fabric. The result is a retreat with a refined spiritual quality.*

Furniture surely holds center stage in a white room, especially if the upholstery is the color of cream, the curtains ivory, and the walls papered in white-on-white damask wallpaper. As with interiors decorated in natural tones, white rooms come to life when there is a variety of texture present. A thick, plush white wool rug played against white diaphanous silk curtains with sleek white-painted walls is much more arresting to the eye than indifferent surfaces all in the same cream tone.

White is versatile, but it may not be for everyone. People who love full-bodied hues may find themselves color-starved in a white room. Others may be put off by its impracticality.

White rooms do show wear and tear more than those of a less fragile color. But people who live in them are willing to put up with the extra maintenance. They say it is a small price for the serenity these airy spaces inspire.

When clients suggest painting walls a color other than white, designer Frank Babb Randolph asks, "Why? White makes furniture look so wonderful." Case in point: Randolph's own house, a tone-on-tone montage of white shapes (above and left). The shagreen coffee table and entryway bench with powdery finish have the qualities Randolph savors. Wall paint is "Designer White" from Pratt & Lambert.

White porcelain fixtures are always designer Paul Vincent Wiseman's choice for the bathroom. In this elegant room (above and opposite), he achieves a luxurious, spa-like feeling by surrounding fixtures with creamy woodwork and marble, then setting the room shimmering with silver accents, mirrors, and frosted glass. The lights over the sink are period gas and electric, with new crystal-fringed shades. A sterling touch is the aluminum chair based on a Thonet design. The walls are painted with Benjamin Moore's Number 950, a creamy ivory color. Because ceilings usually read darker than walls, the ceiling is a slightly lighter ivory tone.

chapter 5

PAINTED SURFACES

The quickest way to dress up a room is to apply the paintbrush. A lick of paint can totally transform a space, turning it sunny (with yellow), romantic (with peach), or avant-garde (with black). Conventional wisdom claims that light colors make small rooms seem larger. But some of the most talented interior designers like deep colors for their space-expanding quality of "pushing" walls back. Painting the woodwork and ceiling a contrasting hue from the walls lends definition to a room's architecture, which is desirable in a space with fine proportions and handsome architectural detailing. Decorative paintwork can bring a single piece of furniture or a whole room to life.

Achieving nuances of tones or unusual colors once required custom-mixing. But today's ready-mixed paints offer literally thousands of choices, making it possible to create rooms in sophisticated hues straight from a can. The many finishes available all have an effect on color. Matte paints dry to a totally dull finish with no shine at all. On a wall, they read darker than the same color will appear when the paint has a glossy finish. Paints with gloss finishes shine like patent leather once they dry; their light-reflecting property tends to lighten colors. Eggshell finishes, with a semi-sheen that is easy to clean, are practical for woodwork.

RICH COLOR
ON A TIGHT BUDGET

A luscious color on the walls gives a room a sumptuous look, even though the furniture may be spare and the budget small. That was the philosophy of the design firm Feldman-Hagan in choosing lavender paint for the bedroom on these pages. Part of a magazine project to show how to put together a stylish room furnished entirely through mail-order catalogs, the situation is instructive for anyone operating on a less than lavish budget.

Victoria Hagan and her late partner, Simone Feldman, paged through dozens of catalogs, and, guided only by photographs, ordered a table here, a bed there, accessories from everywhere. They chose the rich lavender color to fill up the room and hold the disparate mail order furnishings together. The color, Hagan explains, "has just enough punch to keep the room light, soft, and romantic, but it is not as overwhelming as red or blue would be."

Selecting the color was the design team's first decorating decision. The choice was Benjamin Moore's Number 14231A. They tested it by painting a large area of wall, about a square yard or so, and by studying it in daylight and evening light. "It is misleading to go by the small samples," Hagan cautions. She also advises doing a paint test of the intended trim color next to the trial wall patch to be sure that one color doesn't alter the look of the other. On this project, the designers chose a white with a slight bluish cast for the trim ~ crown molding, baseboards, and chair rail ~ that sets off the lavender walls smartly.

Teaming lavender with pink and other cottage pastels would have been the conventional way to decorate with it. But by concentrating on "the way we see lavender in nature," the designers avoided the expected and instead paired the color with the tones of leaves and branches. A natural sisal carpet in tawny tones covers the floor. Commanding center stage is a four-poster bed in metal with a brownish finish. A settee in tan wicker is a main seating piece, and a table draped with a taupe-and-cream blanket in large checks functions as a console against one wall. Celadon green accents are brightening touches.

With so many rough textures ~ the sisal, wicker, and dull metal ~ the designers chose a matte finish for the wall paint. "I usually choose paint finish to relate to the other things in the room," Hagan explains. Here, the finish provides a softness that complements the unshiny surfaces. And in a softly polished contrast, the white trim framing the lavender walls bears a semigloss finish. The result is a quirky, unusual room, neither too precious nor too sweet. "It's mysterious," says Hagan.

The color lavender is usually associated with ruffles and full-blown floral prints. But in this bedroom, the designers achieved a romantic feeling while keeping the room tailored and restrained. Unadorned by bed hangings, the metal four-poster has an unpolished surface that works well with the matte lavender walls.

The gray-green color of
lilac leaves inspired the
selection of accessories ~
baskets made of Scotch
pine are lined up along
the mantel, and on the
table are chargers and
rice bowls of celadon
Chinese pottery (above).

The layering of brown
tones and textures ~
wicker settee, sisal rug,
and pine floorboards ~
keeps the lavender decor
from lapsing into cloying
sweetness and cliché. On
the blanket-draped
console the beige tones of
a classical bust and a
wood flat of spring bulbs
adds to the pleasing
mixture of brown-toned
surfaces (opposite).

96

RECIPE FOR A BRILLIANT KITCHEN

Whenever there is a party at JoAnn Roberts' house, just about everyone ends up in the kitchen, attracted by the joyful medley of vivid colors throughout the room. Roberts, a San Francisco–area designer who specializes in residential remodeling, devised the scheme of saturated hues as an integral part of the redesign of her Edwardian-era kitchen. The original room, surrounded by maids' rooms, was inconveniently located near the back of the house. By borrowing adjacent space, Roberts relocated it so that it would be near the dining room on one side and just off the backyard patio and pool on the other.

The new layout is a step forward on the traditional work triangle. Two large islands dominate the center of the room, providing ample cooking space for the whole family to pull together weekend breakfasts. Other enviable features are a professional refrigerator with brushed stainless-steel doors, a cooking wall at one end of the room that includes a professional range and overhead grill, and a bar counter with plenty of cabinets and drawers for china, glasses, cutlery, and linens. To flood the room with constant daylight,

Roberts cut three 6-foot-square skylights in the ceiling and added two huge 10-by-10-foot picture windows at one end.

Color pulls the room together. For the two large islands, the designer chose scarlet red. Yellow was her choice for tall, narrow cabinets on each side of the cooking range, as well as for the bar counter and the cabinets next to the refrigerator. To achieve brilliant color on the custom-built ash cabinetry with a transparent finish that would let the wood grain show through, she had the painter apply oil-based enamel paint as if it were a stain. It was put on the cabinets with rags, wiped off, and then sealed. Instead of a polyurethane sealer, which might turn yellow, the painter used a water-based sealer that does not change color.

Black is the striking accent: black granite slick as patent leather for the countertops and black laminate with a mottled glossy and matte pattern for the dining table. Around that table Roberts arranged Danish architect Arne Jacobsen's classic 1950s chairs in eight different candy-bright colors.

Such vivid color might have been overwhelming if Roberts had used it on every

Gathering together all the colors used in this California kitchen is a mosaic tile backsplash in shards of licorice black and bright pastels, installed on the far wall behind the cooking range. Splashes of red include the faucet and the fire-engine legs of the black laminate table. The unmatched chairs sport crayon-bright colors.

surface, but she wisely held back. "I love color, but you have to use it sparingly because it's very strong," she explains. To counterbalance it, she covered the walls and ceiling in a creamy eggnog color. But here again the application was unusual: Rather than having the walls painted, Roberts had them done in troweled plaster. With this technique, color pigment is mixed into the plaster before it is applied to the wall. "You get a depth of color you can't get with paint," she explains. "The walls look like suede ~ they're so beautiful you don't want to hang art on them." In this kitchen, the artful use of color is decoration enough.

Color is used to identify the different zones of the kitchen. All the storage cabinetry is yellow, while the cooking and preparation islands are painted bright red. A work island has ample shelves for the owner's collection of cookbooks (left), and a stainless-steel toaster slides out at one end (above left). The bar area, with its rich black granite countertop and yellow cabinets, is stationed near the patio doors (opposite).

A BRUSH
WITH COLOR

Painted furniture and accessories can sometimes completely transform the look of a room. From an eighteenth-century English japanned secretary to a simple painted American country chair, there is a style of painted furniture for every budget.

Taking a paintbrush to a flea-market find or unfinished piece of pine is another way to provide a colorful furniture accent for a room, at the same time offering an opportunity for personal creative expression. For the enterprising furniture decorator, there is a huge range of painted furniture styles from which to borrow ideas. Inspiration can come from old American country chests and boxes decorated in explosive swirls and graining, achieved by manipulating paint with a brush or graining comb. Mustard, barn red, gray, faded teal, or dull green are some authentic colonial hues; many paint companies offer outstanding ready-mixed collections of period colors. Other painted styles worth imitating include Pennsylvania Dutch or Bavarian hearts and flowers motifs, as well

Painted American country furniture like this teal blue table provides a warm note in a room (top). With their large flat surfaces, armoires and cupboards are wonderful canvases for painted decorations. The larger the cupboard, and the more emphatic the paint, the more it will take on the importance of an architectural presence in a room. A blue-and-yellow cupboard with tiny floral bouquets on the doors fills in a spot just under the stairs of a California beach cottage (above). And a boldly painted armoire acts as the focal point in a room with no mantel or other structural details (opposite).

The colorful designs Vanessa Bell painted at Charleston, her English country farmhouse, were done around 1916. Working with slightly grayed hues, she and Duncan Grant, another Bloomsbury artist, made wallpapers of painted stencils. On the fireplace surround in Grant's studio is a tawny-hued human figure and giant compote (left). Cloisonné-like designs painted on a window eclipse the view (below). Hovering above the window is a frieze of coral, yellow, and taupe discs; on either side are trompe l'oeil niches with bloom-filled vases.

as the pastel tones of Scandinavian folk furniture or the warm terracottas and green-blues of Mediterranean decor.

Still another option, with paintbrush in hand, is to let the imagination run wild. The inventiveness of Vanessa Bell is a fine inspiration. Dipping into her own unique wellspring, this artist of the avant-garde Bloomsbury group decorated every room in her farmhouse in the English countryside in riotous color, leaving scarcely a chair or wall untouched, as the photographs here reveal.

Artists, poets, and writers ~ among them Virginia Woolf, Vanessa Bell's sister ~ all came to visit at Charleston. Bell provided the group with a forum for lively conversation by transforming an ordinary round dining table into a fanciful design of orange, yellow, and aqua circular shapes (left).

A voluptuous female nude issues an invitation to bathe (below). Rooms at Charleston were always cold; the warm terracottas and blues and the sportive nude undoubtedly chased winter chills from the morning bath. These are the sunny colors of hot climates, not rainy England.

A specific mood can be established in a room by painting the walls a strong color. Cherry-red walls in a New England kitchen that is the scene of family dinners and lively gatherings seem to symbolize the good cheer of these occasions (above).

The tobacco stripe in a classic chintz inspired the wall color choice in the living room of Mark Hampton's weekend house on Long Island (opposite). The unusually dark color sets a cozy mood in winter; in the summer it is cool and shady. The pediment-top bookcase, the strongest shape in the room, is finished in pale tones that wake up the room and keep the deep brown walls from being gloomy and overpowering.

cha 6 *pter*

FABRICS

Fabric is a great standard bearer of color in interior design. It supplies color to windows, sofas, and chairs, all of which comprise a major group of surfaces in a room. A change of fabric on furniture and curtains can completely refresh a space, even if the paint and wallpaper remain the same. That is the secret of slipcovers' popularity ~ they are a portable investment that can be packed up and moved to the next house or season.

Because of the pliable nature of fabric, which allows it to be draped, tucked, gathered, and shirred, it can have a softening effect on color. As the folds of fabric catch light and shadow, colors subtly shift to lighter and darker tones. With silks and silky finishes, the play of light on color is especially beautiful. The same hue on a fabric with a shiny finish tends to read lighter than it will on a textured one. Those with a nap ~ velvet, corduroy, suede, chenille ~ make color appear both light and dark, depending on which way the pile is brushed; no other fabrics bring color to life quite so dramatically.

HIGH-VOLTAGE PATTERNS
IN A LONDON TOWNHOUSE

In the living room, fabrics in luscious acid fruit colors are played against black wall-to-wall carpeting accessorized by rag rugs in vivid cerulean blue (opposite). The window treatment is Italian silk in stripes of light and dark orange (above). Fabrics in such sunlit colors are a fine choice for curtains because they create a sunny look as the light streams through, turning a room cheerful on even the dullest day.

A fabric designer, Tricia Guild has made her mark as one of decorating's accomplished colorists. In the late 1970s when loft white was the color and minimalism the last word in style, Guild designed a fabric collection in the pastels of an English cottage garden. Using those fabrics, she turned her London townhouse into a thoroughly romantic abode, a look that anticipated the fashion for English country style that swept through the design world five years later.

Now, when the consensus is for pale neutrals, Guild is once again running ahead of the pack, embracing wonderfully charged-up colors. Her move into her present home couldn't have been timed better: Designers Guild, her fabric and home furnishing company, had just started producing new fabric collections in Van Gogh-strength colors. She used them all through the house.

The high-voltage color scheme began with fabric. The designer's initial inspiration was a floral cotton print on a black background, with enormous flowers and leaves in vivid colors of turquoise and jade. "Very quickly, it became quite obvious to me that if I was using that fabric, there were certain strengths of colors that I should use with it," Guild explains. She decided to wrap the fabric on a large sofa that would be placed in the living room, then chose a wall color of equal intensity ~ jade green ~ to stand up to the fabric. The paint color was rubbed on with

111

rags and brushes, layer by layer, in different shades, until the walls took on a jewel-like depth and radiance. An armchair was covered in a silky yellow fabric, a tone-on-tone damask in yellow and peach went on one ottoman, an avocado silk on another. To underscore the clash of colors, the designer applied contrasting piping to the upholstery and introduced decorative pillows and throws in strong colors. For an added zing, she hung luxurious silk blinds in stripes of cantaloupe and passion fruit at the top of the French doors.

Guild repeated the same process in each room: brilliant color on the wall, contrasting and equally vivid fabrics on the furniture and curtains. Every room is painted a different saturated color: The conservatory has Caribbean-pink walls and furniture covered in blue-and-white cotton checks; each chair is piped in neon green cording. Checked fabrics reappear in the master bedroom, but against a background of electric green walls. For Guild's daughter's bedroom, Mediterranean terracotta walls, peach-colored bed hangings, and pillows and a chair covered in periwinkle blue and pink fabrics were chosen.

Since first doing the rooms, Guild has never repainted the walls, but she often changes the fabrics, trying out new curtain ideas and switching the upholstery fabrics. The highly charged colors always work because they share the same intensity. They also keep Guild where she is most comfortable ~ on the cutting edge of style.

The almost zany mix of checked and striped fabrics in the master bedroom hangs together because all the fabrics repeat shades of blue and blue-green. The parrot-green wall color also has enough blue in it to serve as a harmonizing force to the overall decor. All fabric designs are available through Osborne & Little in the United States.

With peach shades and bed curtains and rosy terracotta walls, Guild's daughter's bedroom captures sunlight during the day and glows in evening lamplight. The curtains are fashioned out of hand-painted cotton duck punctuated with haphazardly brushed-on dots of lilac and orange paint.

A MOSAIC OF
EXOTIC TEXTILES

A merchant who journeyed to India on a rug-buying junket came back marveling. The rugs certainly were fine, and he bought many. But what really captured his interest was the decorating feat the Indian rug dealers performed: By draping their striped and patterned dhurrie carpets over stools and tables, they were able to transform the most ordinary room into a jewel-colored haven straight out of *Arabian Nights*.

That story goes a long way in explaining the room on these pages by New York designer David Salomon, whose style relies on layer upon layer of printed fabric, culminating in an opulent and exotic showing of color and pattern.

The stage was set with paint: gray for the walls, white for the woodwork, and sky blue for the ceiling. For a dash of decorative pattern, red-and-blue stencils were traced over the mantel. Next, Salomon arranged the furniture into a balanced floor plan: a loveseat on one side of the fireplace, an easy chair and wicker chair on the other, with a wicker coffee table in the center.

With the bones of the room in place, the designer selected a vivid ethnic grab bag of textiles: American camp blankets, pillows covered in paisley textiles and oriental carpeting, and an Indian dhurrie rug. Treating the camp blankets as instant slipcovers, he draped one over the white loveseat and another over the blue-and-white-checked

"I love old-looking colors and rich heavy tapestry-like things," says designer David Salomon. In this colorful, exotic living room (above and opposite), he turned unmatched camp blankets into informal throws for the upholstery, then finished off with pillows covered with oriental carpeting and Middle Eastern prints.

114

easy chair. Next he added decorative pillows. The dhurrie rug provided one more
spirited pattern.

Although this combination could have created a jumble of squares, swirls, and zigzags,
the effect is very harmonious. The soothing
background of the room itself assures harmony. And all the textiles "have the same qualities and the same colors," Salomon explains.
Red is the predominant background of most
of the fabrics, with bold motifs of cobalt blue
and minor accents of pale yellow, soft green
and black. The repetition of these colors
prevents the mixture of patterns from
becoming a chaotic crazy quilt.

Having pulled his fabrics from the four
corners of the world, Salomon took the same
approach to accessories. In the center of the
mantel, which is the room's focal point, he
placed a brightly painted Italian platter, then
arranged Italian glass bottles and vases in
brilliant blues and greens on each side. On
the fireplace wall he hung three mirrors with
silvery frames of Mexican beaten tinwork,
and on each side he placed an oriental
ceramic garden stool.

But the finishing touch was a stroke of
pure American Yankee practicality: shades
for the windows in crisp blue-and-white
awning-striped cotton.

*Soft bluish-gray walls
and a loveseat covered in
white cotton create a
neutral foil for the room's
mosaic of color-laden
prints and patterns. The
blue-and-red stencils over
the mantel extend the color
scheme to the walls.*

"You can't have a successful colored room without a neutral shade," says designer Greg Jordan. *"You always need something to compare the color with."* He let lemon yellow walls supply the color in this master bedroom, then outfitted the four-poster bed in beige damask and brown-and-white checked cotton (opposite). The French-style armchairs are done in brown-and-white toile de Jouy (above).

CHOICES OF A DIFFERENT STRIPE

Today's decorating marketplace offers an enormous range of fabrics to choose from. Solid ones are available in every color of the rainbow in natural fibers such as cotton and in synthetics such as rayon. Patterned varieties may have a design printed on the cloth surface, as does chintz; or the pattern may be woven into the textile, as it is with a jacquard weave. The type of fabric selected will be dictated to some degree by the intended use. Heavier fabrics are ideal for upholstery because of their durability; lighter fabrics such as cottons and silks are a fine choice for curtains, seasonal slipcovers, and upholstery that doesn't get hard wear.

A room done mostly in solids tends to have a subdued character. A textured design in the fabric can add visual interest ~ for example, a tone-on-tone damask or stripe.

Patterned fabrics inject energy into a decorating scheme. The combination of garden colors and flower and leaf shapes makes floral prints a favorite choice. There are thousands of florals to pluck for a room, ranging from sweet cottage garden prints of pansies to sophisticated motifs of full-blown tropical orchids. Nonflorals also offer a variety of designs, from a sporty horses-and-hounds print to a repeat of overscale blue-and-white Chinese vases or a witty pattern of teapots, ladies' hats, or winsome cherubs.

Geometrics are another attractive group of patterned fabrics; the most familiar are

stripes, checks, and plaids. Always smart and tailored, they introduce color and pattern without being as intrusive as prints might sometimes be. Mixed with other patterns, a check or a stripe supplies tension and graphic interest.

Selecting a fabric from swatches can be confusing, as they are often too small to allow a fair assessment of the color. It is worth purchasing a yard or so to hang by a window or drape over a sofa in order to evaluate how the color looks in daylight and artificial light, and how the color will look with other fabrics and surfaces.

Designer Beverly Ellsley created a country feeling in a family kitchen with the old-fashioned charm of checks ~ blue-and-white cotton on the armchair, marigold-and-white on the sofa (opposite).

In a Caribbean vacation retreat twin beds are unconventionally dressed in floral bedspreads with different backgrounds (below). Striped shams supply extra pizzazz.

The flea-market origin of
the furniture in this living
room is completely
camouflaged by loose-
fitting slipcovers. Designer
Vicente Wolf chose blue as
the unifying element, then
selected fabrics in shades
ranging from periwinkle
to cadet. By using a
subdued color range and
minimizing pattern (the
blue-and-white stripe on
the pillow is the only one
in the room), he turned a
once motley group of
discards into a pleasingly
harmonious seating
arrangement.

122

chapter 7

ACCESSORIES

Accessories, from lamps to flowers to whimsical personal collections, are the final strokes that bring a decorating scheme to life. A room with the most beautiful curtains and the downiest upholstery may still look flat without the right final touches to inject it with warmth and spirit.

Because they are for the most part movable, accents and accessories can reflect the seasons or changing personal whim. If the walls and furnishings of a room are neutral, it is easy to introduce new colors merely by pulling out certain objects and temporarily retiring others. In rooms with less neutral schemes ~ say, bright red walls or deep green wallpaper ~ accessories of distinctive colors, very light, very dark, or boldly contrasting, can serve to energize the decorating agenda.

Success with accessories takes experimentation. The dash of color that makes a room click can come from anywhere ~ an inexpensive poster, a flea-market vase, a forgotten figurine stashed at the back of a cupboard. It might even come from a grocery store bag of green apples arranged in a favorite bowl.

Two tradesman's signs ~
a bigger-than-life watch,
seen through the doorway,
and a giant pencil ~

are wonderful examples
of accessories with a sense
of humor. Pratt &
Lambert's "Naples

Cream" paint on the
walls shows off the objects'
shapes and antique
painted surfaces.

SHOWCASE FOR ANTIQUES

In the entrance hall, purple delphiniums and lavender-blue nineteenth-century English carpet balls are gentle accents of color against the honey tones of the antique table and Victorian childrens' chairs.

Marston Luce, one of Washington, D.C.'s, leading antiques dealers, has always favored soft, serene colors. His love of the subdued guided the design choices he and Julie Southworth made in restoring their 1920s Washington house, shown here. By simplifying the original architecture, opening up the rooms, and bringing in natural light, the couple created a spare contemporary setting for a wonderful collection of American and European antiques amassed over the past 20 years.

So that nothing in the decor detracted from the antiques themselves, Luce and Southworth kept the colors neutral and the rooms almost completely devoid of pattern. Walls and ceilings in the living and dining rooms are cream with a tinge of pink and beige, and the pine floors throughout the house were bleached to a pale beige. In the entrance hall, the floorboards were scored with a diamond motif, and small black squares were painted where the diamonds meet. Even the modern upholstery is unobtrusive: For the living room, the couple chose overstuffed pieces in traditional shapes, then had them covered in beige and cream-colored fabrics that virtually fade into the walls.

With the neutral stage set, Luce and Southworth next brought on the antique furniture. American country Chippendale chairs from the early 1800s slid under the Federal table in the dining room. A French chest was placed in the living room near the sofa; beside it, an English neo-Gothic hall chair.

Upstairs went the couple's prized possession: an antique Regency chest, covered in its original robin's-egg-blue paint.

But it is the antique accessories, carefully placed throughout the rooms, that give the interiors resonance and the witty touch of the designers' personalities. Propped on the French chest in the living room is a huge gilt-painted nineteenth-century wooden watch, part of a shop sign that once hung outside a watchmaker's shop in Quebec. Leaning

Jewel tones come together in an arrangement of cherished objects clustered around an English William IV fruitwood table. Taking center stage is a nineteenth-century Hudson River School painting; the rich greens and golds of the majestic landscape are enhanced by the gilded frame. Underneath the painting is a French bouillotte lamp with a shade in deep green tole.

Very soft colors create a romantic mood in the bathroom. Walls are dressed in a printed paper of pale blue and white and decorated with watercolors of seashells in fragile beige tones. On an antique bamboo commode prances a winsome little cherub figure, its painted wood surface gently worn. Gilded frames on the mirror and watercolors provide a burnished sparkle.

against the dining room wall is another trades-man's sign ~ an enormous pencil that was dis-played outside a pencil factory in the early part of this century. Exhibited like paintings, these pieces have an amusing quality that keeps the rooms from seeming staid. More serious pieces include an exquisite nineteenth-century French mirror with carved wood frame painted in gold and seafoam blue that graces the entrance, and numerous portraits and land-scapes appear on walls throughout the house. Charming pieces like the diminutive neo-Gothic Victorian childrens' chairs grouped in the entrance hall and the carved wooden putto whimsically poised in the bathroom provide the finishing touches.

Unmatched blue tones on a painted chair, slipper chair, and loveseat pillows lend the bedroom a casual air.

A PASSION FOR COLLECTING

Shared rosy tones tie together new bone china service plates with antique lusterware bread-and-butter plates on a dinner table (above).

Understated richness reigns on the wall: A dazzling giltwood mirror, with black candles in its sconces, is flanked by pencil drawings framed in gold and green (opposite).

Absolutely exquisite accessories are one of the hallmarks of Susan Zises Green's self-taught style. A wonderful showcase for the interior designer's work is the New York City apartment she decorated for herself, her husband, and her two children. A triplex, the Green home is less like an apartment than an elegant little townhouse. The serene harmony of a cream, beige, and sage green scheme enhances its handsome woodwork, high ceilings, and pleasing proportions.

The colors unfold most dramatically in the living room. The green band painted on a nineteenth-century French giltwood mirror inspired the green walls. Mottled with cheesecloth after it was brushed on the walls, the custom-mixed paint has a shiny, glazed finish that sets off the many gilded frames of prints, paintings, and mirrors in the room. The dark green is also a striking contrast to the furniture, all of which is covered in fabrics of cream and beige. Beige silk curtains billow to the floor like the skirts of rustling ball gowns; the carpeting is beige with a pale blue pattern. In the dining room, walls are golden wheat; the sage green appears as a subtle accent in the two curtain fabrics.

The color combination is a superb backdrop for the objects Green has collected over the past 25 years. Many pieces of a huge collection of majolica are displayed in a bamboo-trimmed hutch in the dining room. Pieces of eighteenth-century silk and hand-

Mirrors in almost every room reflect the pale cream and green. The oval mirror (top left) is English. Green trim on the French mirror over the mantel inspired the living room wall color (top right).

With its emphatic mauve, pink, yellow, green, and turquoise tones, an exceptional collection of antique majolica makes a bountiful display against the bamboo-trimmed cabinet (above left).

A black marble tabletop is a dramatic stage for pale accessories (above right). The little birdhouse is an antique creamware potpourri vessel; the elaborate urn-shaped container is English.

The designer's collection of antique accessories includes a number of exceptional urns and vases in light and dark colors, and in every material from porcelain to toleware. Tucked into a niche on the stairway is a metalwork urn filled with metal flowers, one of a pair that came from a grand old movie palace. Tulips spill from a garden urn on a round table at the foot of the stairs. The beige walls are scored to resemble limestone blocks.

blocked chintz have been stitched into pillows. The gentle pinks, greens, browns, and mustards of these period fabrics are radiant on the creamy sofa.

Over the years, Green has developed a taste for other types of accessories as well. She loves round mirrors with carved frames of giltwood; several striking examples dazzle like golden suns on the walls. She collects chairs with unusual carved and painted ornamentation and uses them as accents among the upholstered furniture. She also loves old painted toleware; elegant French pieces in

black and rich gold are arranged throughout the living room and dining room, but the stars of the collection are a pair of metalwork pineapples poised on elaborate tole stands resting on the sideboard in the dining room. "I can't resist painted pieces with a touch of whimsy," she confesses.

The overall effect of these rooms is "mellow, quiet, and restful ~ with a lot of interesting things to look at." Thanks to the soft beige and green background, those things, gathered in a lifetime of collecting, are a prominent part of the decor for all to enjoy.

ADDING THE PERSONAL TOUCH

"Instant heritage" is designer Mario Buatta's term for one-stop accessorizing ~ which he abhors. Rather, he advises, accessorizing should be a slow process in which objects are added "a dab at a time," with the final result appearing "as if things were accumulated over a lifetime."

In a room with a well-planned color scheme, accessories take on the very important role of carrying the color message to all areas of the room. Personal taste, as much as the style of the room, dictates the choice of finishing touches: For a tailored contemporary mood, mostly black and gray items might be the way to go. For a lively, cheerful room, vividly colored lamp bases, artwork, and pillows would be fine choices.

Selecting accessories can be a delightful treasure hunt. Antiques shops, flea markets, and fine design stores all may yield the prize. If it comes down to a costly object, it is wise to try it out before making a financial commitment. The best antiques shops usually allow objects to be taken home "on approval" if there is a question about getting scale, proportion, and color right, but a flea-market vendor may not be so accommodating. Searching out accessories of the right color, shape, and texture requires patience, a willingness to experiment, and a sense of fun. And when the object turns up in just the right shade ~ usually in the least expected place ~ it is a trophy well worth the search.

Designer Carolyn Guttilla grouped several shades of white around a white chest to create a romantic vignette (above).

In the same house, in a play of contrasts, a lineup of metal ornaments forms a frieze of silhouetted shapes against a pastel-toned 1920s travel poster (opposite).

134

In a New York City apartment dominated by vanilla walls, pale woods, and clean-lined modern furniture, neutral accessories predominate (above). On the blond wood table in the foreground, a wooden shoemaker's form steps in as a witty sculpture.

Golden embellishments inject warmth in even the sparest interior. Designer Craig Raywood added sparkle to an arrangement of nineteenth-century antiques with a mirror in a burnished frame and a round table banded in gold (above right).

A French armchair upholstered in oxblood leather becomes a formidable accent piece in Raywood's hands, robust enough for the black painting on the wall and the blue china lamp on the desk (above).

A *careful arrangement of cream, beige, and metallic accessories imparts a soft appearance to a vanity table. The photograph of graveyard statuary is framed in white wood; the white vase in the foreground displays a satyr-like visage. Adding to the idiosyncratic character of the accessories is a white garden chair with a rusted metal finish.*

Tones of butterscotch, bittersweet, camel, and black are woven into the color blocks of a fringed throw draped on a white sofa. The spicy colors are repeated in the black and camel tiles of the table and the little terracotta figurine.

In a room with refined traditional manners, golden finishes can be especially beautiful, throwing into relief the decorative raised surfaces and sinuous shapes of the antique pieces on display. A notable example is the living room in the country house of designer Mark Hampton; its dense, chocolate-colored walls serve as a wonderful background for golden objects (above left). The room's most stunning element is the giltwood English Regency triptych mirror over the mantel; reflected in it are nineteenth-century gilt-bronze candlesticks.

A giltwood frame accentuates the curves of a shapely little Victorian slipper chair (above right). Echoing the full-blown flowers of the chair's needlepoint upholstery is a bouquet of blooming roses resting on a table. A leaf-shaped plate adds a dash of emerald richness to the tablescape.

Wide white mats and
narrow frames of dark
wood on a vibrant blue
wall unify a group of
prints in the apartment
of designer Katie Ridder
and architect Peter
Pennoyer (left).

*In a room designed by
Eric Cohler, a yellow vase
filled with red tulips gives
punch to an arrangement
of photographs and books
with leather bindings and
vintage covers (above).
In another grouping, the
designer paired tribal
masks and a formal
antique portrait, letting
the harmony between the
brown tones in both tie
them together (left). Ruby-
red walls provide a dra-
matic backdrop.*

DIRECTORY OF
DESIGNERS AND ARCHITECTS

Linda Banks
Norwalk, Connecticut

Byron Bell
New York, New York

Ward Bennett
New York, New York

Nancy Braithwaite
Atlanta, Georgia

Mario Buatta
New York, New York

Eric Cohler
New York, New York

Robert Currie
New York, New York

Beverly Ellsley
Westport, Connecticut

Susan Zises Green
New York, New York

Tricia Guild
London, England

Pat Guthman
Southport, Connecticut

Carolyn Guttilla
Locust Valley, New York

Victoria Hagan
New York, New York

Mark Hampton
New York, New York

Greg Jordan
New York, New York

Robert Kleinschmidt
Chicago, Illinois

Sheila Camera Kotur
New York, New York

Jorge Letelier
New York, New York

Marston Luce
Washington, D.C.

Mark McInturff
Washington, D.C.

Lee Mindel
New York, New York

David Mitchell
Washington, D.C.

Stephen Muse
Washington, D.C.

Peter Pennoyer
New York, New York

Frank Babb Randolph
Washington, D.C.

Craig Raywood
New York, New York

Michael Rex
Sausalito, California

Katie Ridder
New York, New York

JoAnn Roberts
Hillsborough, California

Michael Rubin
New York, New York

John Saladino
New York, New York

David Salomon
New York, New York

Peter Shelton
New York, New York

Mark Simon
Bethesda, Maryland

Julie Southworth
Washington, D.C.

Jeanne Taylor
Greenwich, Connecticut

Ron Wilson
Los Angeles, California

Paul Vincent Wiseman
San Francisco, California

Vicente Wolf
New York, New York

The room on page 11 was designed by Greg Jordan; page 16, Robert Kleinschmidt; page 36, John Saladino; page 58, Linda Banks; page 74, Jeanne Taylor; page 124, Stephen Muse.

PHOTOGRAPHY CREDITS

1	David Montgomery	61-63	Jeff McNamara	103	Lilo Raymond
7	Langdon Clay	64-69	Langdon Clay	104-105	Michael Dunne
11	Jeff McNamara	70	Antoine Bootz	106	Karen Radkai
15	Kari Haavisto	71	Judith Watts	107	Lizzie Himmel
16	Scott Frances	72	Kari Haavisto	108	David Montgomery
18-21	Langdon Clay	73	Antoine Bootz	110-113	David Montgomery
22-25	Judith Watts	74	Judith Watts	114-117	Antoine Bootz
26	Antoine Bootz	76	Jeff McNamara	118-119	Jeff McNamara
28-31	Antoine Bootz	78-79	Jeff McNamara	120	Kari Haavisto
32-33	Jeff McNamara	80-85	Langdon Clay	121	Lisl Dennis
34	Michael Dunne (top)	86	Antoine Bootz	122-123	Jeff McNamara
	Kari Haavisto (bottom)	87	John Vaughan	124	Walter Smalling
35	Jeff McNamara	88	Langdon Clay	126-129	Walter Smalling
36, 38	Antoine Bootz	89	Gordon Beall	130-133	Thibault Jeanson
40-47	Antoine Bootz	90-91	John Vaughan	134-135	Kari Haavisto
48	Elyse Lewin	92	Michael Dunne	136	Jeff McNamara (top left)
50-53	Elyse Lewin	95-97	Antoine Bootz		Antoine Bootz (top and
54	Antoine Bootz	98	David Duncan		bottom right)
55	Langdon Clay		Livingston	137	Jeff McNamara
56	David Phelps	100-101	David Duncan	138	Lizzie Himmel
57	Lilo Raymond (top)		Livingston	139	Antoine Bootz (top)
	Walter Smalling	102	Michael Skott (top)		Jacques Dirand
	(bottom)		Tim Street-Porter		(bottom and right)
58	Jeff McNamara		(bottom)		

*House Beautiful would like to thank the following homeowners:
Joan and Robert Infarinato (page 15), Kiki Boucher and
Aaron Shipper (pages 22-25), Nat Hirsch (page 55), Tricia Foley
(page 86), Gina and Mike Cerre (page 87), Nini Reeves (page 106),
Liz Pringle (page 121), Elke Kasman and Bob Sanger (pages
134-135), Dara Caponigro (pages 136-137).*